M000315688

LIVING INSPIRED™
WITH LUMARI

Engage the Lights of Awakening,
Revelation and Transformation

Lumari

LIVING INSPIRED™ WITH LUMARI
Engage the Lights of Awakening, Revelation and Transformation

LUMARI
www.Lumari.com

ISBN - 978-0-9679553-2-2

 Amethyst

Get more joy in your life!

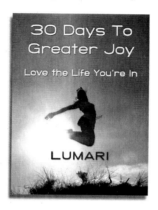

Free download!

30 DAYS TO GREATER JOY
Love the Life You're In

Discover simple, fun, actionable ways to bring more joy into your life!

- Move from mundane to magical
- Embrace your life and live inspired
- Take action to create more instant joy and ease

30 DAYS TO GREATER JOY

Get the free download here!
http://www.lumari.com/joy.html

Your joy momentum begins as soon as you do!

To Peter, my beloved,
who endlessly inspires me to celebrate the moment
with love and laughter.

About The Author

Lumari is gifted as an internationally known Visionary Energy Master, Intuitive Coach, Healer and Author helping her clients, celebrate their soul purpose, fulfill their dreams, follow their highest path of destiny and Live Inspired.

With clients all over the world, she serves as a catalyst, guide and inspiration for personal, professional and planetary change, healing, evolution and transformation to teach her clients to Align with the Divine, Build their Business, Change the World and Live Inspired.

Enjoying a successful career as a sculptor, Lumari integrated her gifts as an artist with her powerful intuitive gifts of vision, channeling and communication to relentlessly follow her vision and spiritual guidance and serve as a coach and spiritual teacher for Leaders, Creatives, Healers and Innovators.

She breaks apart preconceived ideas of personal growth, spiritual awakening and fulfilling your destiny so you can be the joyful soul and spirit you know you are inside.

To Live Inspired, contact Lumari at www.LUMARI.com.

Other Books by Lumari

Akashic Records: Collective Keepers of Divine Expression introduces you to The Keepers of the Akashic, the beings of the ancient collective who gather and contain all universal knowledge. She brings the wisdom of the ages into the clarity of now. Her book is required reading for many study courses about the Akashic.

ALAWASHKA - the Original Language and Vibrational Source of Creation, channeled by Lumari, reveals the nature of Creation, the evolution of humanity and the power of our original sacred language. This book is a powerful and uplifting exploration of creation, healing and new spiritual awakening that can help you awaken to new frequencies of light and healing that will change your life and our world.

Lumari's Guide to Crystals and Gems - Unlocks the secrets of over 200 gemstones to increase your health, harmony, happiness and more. This Guide contains over 580 pages of gemstone wisdom that gives you easy, clear access to the powerful spiritual, magical and healing properties of gems, stones and crystals.

Visit **www.Amazon.com** and **www.Lumari.com** for more information about these books.

Contents

LIVING INSPIRED™ WITH LUMARI
Engage the Lights of Awakening, Revelation and Transformation

Preface:

Active Inspiration

I wrote this book to reclaim the word, essence, and active spirit of inspiration.

Someone stole the word "inspiration" and left it to sputter in a soft romantic illusion. Somewhere the power of this word vanished and all of its meaning and magic was left to whither, to dissolve into cliché. Time retranslated the word into a passive state and the power that inspiration brings, the power to consciously change the world, was dissolved.

And when the true meaning of this word was stolen, it was as though no one had access to participating with inspiration. No one had access to the gifts of actively engaging with inspiration. This is personal. So it's time to reclaim inspiration and then to empower its truth and wisdom.

This book will heal the misconceptions of inspiration and ignite those energies with a new, dynamic force. The visions for this book and the reasons for writing and exploring this divine gift are to help you:

- Discover the unlimited source of your personal wisdom and brilliance

- Experience profound joy, fulfillment, creative possibility, inspired actions and results

- Find your calling, shine a light on your true passion and contribute to the world in truly meaningful ways

- and then to *Live Inspired*!

I have a passion and connection with inspiration.

If this is our first meeting: "Welcome! It's great to meet you." If you've read some of my other books, joined a teleseminar, attended one of my workshops, or met me in person:

"Delighted to connect with you again."

I train visionary leaders, healers, artists, creatives, and innovators to Align with the Divine, Build their Businesses, and Change the World. I've authored several books, and I serve as a catalyst and guide for personal, professional, and planetary change, healing, evolution, and awakening.

The energy of this book tantalized me even before I finished leading my last group seminar, Heal Your Money Karma. The full force of inspiration came to me during the seminar and I announced the next group seminar, called Living Inspired. This book arises from that work.

The creative and the intuitive spiritual processes both rely on inspiration. I am very attentive to that process, and I bring inspiration to me. I have many different ways of tuning in and being open to inspiration and the creative process. As I explored the wisdom of the ages and the divine frequencies, I discovered a whole world of inspiration that I knew, but no one else seemed to recognize. I always traveled in this world as an artist, never realizing that I was traveling in the spiritual realms of inspiration.

As I explored inspiration to reveal it and teach it, I realized I have a different relationship and understanding of the word, meaning, process, and engagement with inspiration. I am *Living Inspired* while most people are waiting to be *inspired*. I realized that most people don't even think of or consider inspiration as a means of expression. And those who do are waiting for inspiration to find them. They are waiting for the moment when inspiration brings them magic.

Well, that motivated me to write, to explore, to unravel this confusion so I could free and empower inspiration.

I felt like inspiration was being hijacked. The power and beauty of inspiration was being held hostage in misconception and illusion. Inspiration—my dear friend, my spirit guide, and an ancient, wise, and beautiful partner in my life—was being kidnapped, and I had to do something. That's how this book evolved.

How can I coach, teach, and train people who want to grow into their "soul purpose" and are ready to step into a brighter, more powerful, prosperous, and successful spirit-led future, when inspiration is being misappropriated? How can people soar and create wonder and uplift and change our world when they are waiting for inspiration to happen to them?

So I am reclaiming the word, essence, vibration, and active spirit of inspiration. I'm taking it back for all of us! I invite you to actively pursue and engage inspiration in your life.

Most people give up on inspiration. They wait for the influence, the light of a guiding force to encourage their path. They wait for the brilliant spark that begins as a flame and becomes a torch lighting their way. And if that inspiration doesn't materialize, if it doesn't appear, then they do not feel and connect with that brilliance.

I want to liberate the word and experience of inspiration from the passive confines of waiting for divine intervention. I want to bring it out of the lethargy of romantic and sentimental inaction.

I wrote this book to reveal, to share, and to encourage you to go beyond the preconceived notions and ideas of inspiration. I want you to flourish with light, joy, and beauty and bring all of that into whatever you do and however you live. So, Living Inspired with Lumari is infused with powerfully positive vibrations and blessings designed to raise your energy and perspective so you can connect with your own higher aspects of pure inspiration. These vibrations are woven into the words and poetry of this book and when you are ready, you will realize, acknowledge and align with your next levels of beauty, transformation and fulfillment.

The blessings and frequencies encoded in this book are designed on a personal level to encourage, revitalize and strengthen you in your growth, joy and purpose. They will engage your soul purpose, guide your destiny and uplift and transform your life. On a universal level these sacred frequencies are designed to impart blessings into our world.

Each time you read and reread a section or favorite passage, you will be able to shift into a higher level of your own beauty, gifts and soul path, so you can celebrate your life and actively share the blessings of Living Inspired.

How will this look in your life? You may realize a bond of oneness. You may have deep and powerful insights that lead to personal transformation. You may shift your perspective and abilities to manifest your dreams. You may find new focus and passion or rekindle your past dreams into real successes. You may find more love. You may discover your heart's calling and awaken to a deeper, richer part of your soul. You may experience personal and emotional healing and clearing that brings greater meaning, joy and fulfillment, just by reading this book.

In my Living Inspired with Lumari group coaching program, the results were astounding. One person met the love of her life, during our coaching program. This fabulous over-forty business woman finally found her soul mate and is starting a new, enriching, and creative life.

Another person found true joy in the most difficult year of her life. She thought joy was beyond her and really that joyful people were probably lying or deluding themselves. Now, she is filled with grounded, real joy every day. A writer and dancer in this coaching program is creating her dreams and visions with rapid speed, writing and choreographing a new play, and creating with amazing results and surprising support. These are three examples of the power and joyful transformation Living Inspired and the frequencies and teachings this book imparts and brings.

This book reclaims the magic, mystery, and motivation of inspiration so you can engage with it. Together, we can lift it from the passive and bring the action back into it.

It's time to interact with it, invite it, unleash it.

I invite you to start *Living Inspired*.

The Sacred Story:

A Summer Night

Early in the evening on a sweet summer night, Maya sat looking at the distant stars. It was a long day. It was a good life. Memories flowed like wine to her heart. She sighed an end-of-the-day sigh. It was an end-of-a-cycle sigh. Something was missing. Life was good, and yet something was missing.

Smiling, patiently sitting just across from her, three angels chatted.

"Just hit her with your halo. That should do it," one angel laughed.

"Shush! Don't say that out loud. You know I've tried that before and it didn't work. I actually placed it over her head, just to see if she would notice. Nothing. Who doesn't notice a halo?"

The second angel poked her in the ribs and laughed. "I know. I've sent her so many messages. Hello? Sweetheart! Wake up."

The third angel just shook her head. "It's so sad."

The other two angels turned. Their friend rose off of the bench across from Maya.

"She doesn't know. This is made for her. She doesn't see. She isn't open to it and it's breaking my heart. "

She held a carved sapphire box, the lid fastened to guard a most precious gift. Rainbow sparked light danced inside the box, containing a secret brilliance as yet to be revealed.

The other angels stood on either side of her.

"You know we have to go."

"I know. Can we try one more time?"

The three angels looked at the sapphire box and smiled.

"Should we?"

"No rules against it? No one else is here to see it revealed."

"On the count of three?"

They nodded in unison.

One. Two. Three.

They opened the box and streams of light danced, shot out of the gemstone box and scattered across the sky. Brilliant prisms proclaimed themselves across the stars like soundless fireworks in celebration. The angels eagerly looked at Maya sitting in her chair.

Then she sighed. The angels looked at her in hopeful anticipation.

"I guess I'll go in now. I have a busy day tomorrow," Maya said as she pushed herself off of the chair.

The angels bowed their heads and vanished into the Cosmic All.

Their gifts of inspiration, yet again, left unnoticed.

PART 1:

Awaiting the Brilliance

One Dream

One dream running in silent footfall
Darting through a sacred moment in time
Carrying the eternal flame
Breathless, laughing in the deep blue
of endless cosmic nights
Eager for your smile of recognition to dance
in delight and promise

Streaming across the skies. Magic. Power. Wonder.
Searchlight chasing a dream, carrying a vision
in a crystal jar
Gifts to last a lifetime

Divine huntress with a golden falcon seeking the voice,
the spark, the reciprocal vibration that echoes a
response
in hearts joyful
Where are they? Where are you?

The eternal flame flickers
The voice becomes an unanswered echo
Inspiration asks, "Where were you?"

Distracted, indifferent, unmindful
Vacant eyes stare into the heart of brilliance and see nothing

Chapter 1:

Divine Invitation

Inspiration is divine communication and invitation. The Divine, a gracious and endless being through which universes rise into light and disperse into the cosmic night, calls to you. She sends a light, an exclusive message, to you. This brilliance begins as a whisper, sweetly touching you and asking you to play. "Will you come and play? Will you join this sacred dance? I have wonders and beauty to share with you."

A shimmer, a breeze, and a soft electric pulse moves within you. Can you feel it? Do you recognize it? Most inspiration sent to you goes unnoticed. It lingers and then dissipates. And you don't notice, and you don't know that you are supposed to notice.

Many people have a complete misconception of inspiration. They do not even think of inspiration at all. They do not expect to be inspired because it doesn't even occur to them. They are completely unaware. You are reading this book because you cherish and would like to experience more inspiration in your life.

The misconceptions about inspiration are many. It's time to burst apart the illusions about inspiration and suspend the ideas of a whimsical, capricious muse of inspiration that most likely will pass you by, if you even notice it. I love to share a new way of active participation with inspiration that can change your life and uplift our world. I want to open the way for you to recognize inspiration and have a deep and powerful understanding of it. Then fully engage it. Are you ready to explore and play?

What if every day of your life held inspiration? That is Living Inspired. What if every moment you could live from that sacred place and generate your life? Imagine the deep joy you will have when you are fulfilling your higher purpose, guided by the inspired light that you engaged. You are no longer in the passenger seat, waiting and hoping for the divine illumination to grace you with a burst of wisdom. You are in the driver's seat of a Maserati, cruising at joyful speeds to your own inspired destiny. That is Living Inspired.

The ART of Living Inspired is a blessing and an opportunity. It is Awakening, Revelation, and Transformation. Living Inspired is action. You can have inspiration as a conscious, accessible, and active force in every area of your life. You can pursue it, embrace it, and live from that divine place. Be open to access inspiration. Take action to pursue it. Recognize all of the different ways and opportunities you have and can imagine to meet the place of wonder.

No more waiting for the inspiration to hit you. Did you know you could wait all of your life? You know, some people do. You also know that in this waiting, you are missing an opportunity to connect, to forge a new relationship with the Divine, the Goddess, the Creatrix, the One Spirit of All.

You can become the banquet for inspiration. Invite the guests, the messengers, the vision, the connection. Cater the party with all of the attributes as the delicacies you will savor and enjoy. Bring in the music of your heart and soul. Dance, and celebrate the sacred harmonies that keep creativity, wonder, and love flowing.

Living Inspired is actively engaging in and pursuing inspiration in your own life. This connects you to Spirit in a conscious dialogue. Inspiration ignites our brilliance in a way that changes us and changes our world. It is the easiest way to make changes because the nature of inspiration changes us. It opens your heart and invites you into a space of collaboration so that your light shines a new light to others, and together we will uplift and change our world!

Inspiration evokes brilliant ideas, flashes of light and energy, and something truly momentous. Out of nowhere, in the space of an instant, we are impressed by something and our reality shifts. This experience is life-altering and life-changing. In a flash something happens to us and we see the world through a whole new light. This is an extraordinary experience.

This is a brilliant occurrence where something in our lives, something seemingly indefinable, touches us, impresses us, and moves us in a way that stops time. We are caught in an eternal moment when life stills and the new, vibrant energy of inspiration awakens us to something else, something bigger than our own self. You can sense the energy change.

Inspiration is a positive, heartfelt, intuitive direction that uplifts, awakens, transforms, and enlightens. Inspiration does not cause harm. Right up front, I want to declare that you are never inspired to harm anyone. So before anyone tries to abscond with the word and meaning of inspiration— NO!

Inspiration is a positive blessing that brings you new meaning, joy, freedom, and awakening. It lifts you into curiosity and discovery. It takes you on a swift light-filled journey that changes your perspective and adds to your life.

You want this! You want to feel moved by the flow of brilliance that floods you with wonder.

You want to feel this brilliance and follow where inspiration leads.

Where does it lead? It leads to the greatest minds. It leads to the most amazing art. It leads to the depths of spiritual connection. It leads to the most heartfelt music. It leads to new innovations and discoveries. It leads to profound conversations and relatedness. It leads to new ways of healing and helping. It leads to collaborations for peace and cooperation. It leads to new ways to foster sustainability, organic farming, environmental health, community action, and global awareness.

So, right now, take a breath. Get ready to be open to *be inspired* first. *Being inspired* is the state of letting the brilliance touch you and awaken something more in you.

Then I would love to reveal a whole new way of thinking about inspiration that makes it even bigger and more accessible. I want to open the gateways for you to *live inspired*. *Living Inspired* is actively engaging the forces of inspiration and consciously being the cause of your inspiration.

Thank you for joining this amazing ride!

Inspiration is a very visceral divine message and communication. When you think something is missing in your life, what is missing is inspiration. When you wonder if there is more to your life than what is present right now, then the "more" of your life is inspiration.

Inspiration is a gift and a relationship with the Divine. This is sacred communication. The Divine lifts your eyes and heart to see beyond the single life you have and shares a vision that reaches beyond the moment into the eternal. She gives you an opportunity to connect with the Cosmic All and give back, participating in the joyful expression of light that is uniquely your own. Inspiration brings fullness to your light. It expands the brilliance of your gifts and your special place in the All. It provides the spark to create more than you can see.

This is very distinctly personal and spiritual. It is a sacred message. The Goddess of Inspiration sends you specific vibrations that move you to greatness. One moment of true inspiration lifts your eyes above the horizons of the everyday and unveils a thousand suns shining for you. Every light brings a new brilliance that you can follow, explore, and actualize to expand your own soul purpose and give voice to joyful expression.

These messages come in all ways, ways that are meant for you personally. She knows the heights and depths of your being and communicates directly with you, to share greater gifts than you see at the moment so you can grow into your fullness. She sends messages aligned with your soul purpose and destiny. They are in full harmony with your greater dreams and your soul's quest to resonate with the highest spirit and fulfill your personal quest while you uplift the world in your own unique way. Your inspiration can motivate you to see in new ways, explore new ideas, share your brilliance, and become "the more of you."

Chapter 2:

Living Inspired

L iving Inspired is a new concept that changes how you view and pursue inspiration. Inspiration itself is a pure motivator. It gets things done. It moves perspective. It awakens you to new opportunities and new circumstances in life. Living Inspired is an exponential amplifier that allows you to get inspired. You can stop waiting for the moment, stop waiting for the muse, for the perspective, and go and actively pursue it and then live in those frequencies.

When you engage in and connect with inspiration as an active participant instead of waiting and hoping for inspiration to happen, you connect with your passion, power, and possibility on a whole new level. You connect with and activate your soul purpose in a deliberate, conscious and profound manner.

While divine inspiration is a gift, that still doesn't mean you have to wait for someone to show up at the door, ring the bell, and then hand it over to you. You can go shopping! You can go shopping for your gift. Okay, I do love shopping and if shopping isn't your word, then think seeking, looking, traveling, playing, or exploring. The point is you are engaging with the magic of inspiration. Go shopping for your gift. Find the gifts, vision, wonders, and the compelling reasons that make inspiration worthy, important, and meaningful enough for you to go out looking for it.

The universe, the Divine, has open arms, and when you are Living Inspired you are taking the steps to meet the Divine and embrace Her. She has gifts for you. When you go shopping for your gifts, you are simply saving her the trouble of getting in the cosmic, inter-dimensional jet and finding you to deliver them.

The Difference Between Being Inspired and Living Inspired

Being inspired: When you are being inspired, the actions are triggered in a way that you have to wait for the connection to come to you. Until right now, being inspired was all that was available to you. If you wanted inspiration in your life, that was what you prayed to have happen. Now, it's still absolutely fabulous. There is magic and beauty and wonder in all of it. And yet, to be inspired you still have to wait for the right place, right time, and right circumstance for the universe to recognize you and gift you with inspiration.

Being inspired is passive. Inspiration seizes you. In a way, it holds you captive to its attention and energy. It is a whimsical process, meaning you are at the whim of inspiration—of the energies coming to you, lifting you up, showing you something new. Again, please no judgment, just discernment. You want inspiration, and when it comes this way the surprise of the Divine is gorgeous.

Living Inspired is active. You are the cause. You are involved in the creation of inspiration. You are stepping right in and participating with the universe, taking it all into yourself in a conscious active way, and then you live from that place. You step into the world, your own world with the full garden shining inside you.

You are led by inspiration as a guiding force within you, not outside you or at the whim of the universal. Living Inspired is from the inside out, not the outside in. You embrace the brilliance of your being and invite the universe in to share. What a party that is!

Now the changes you make direct the actions you take.

Sharing Inspiration With You

I should have a bumper sticker that says, "I brake for inspiration."

Inspiration brings out the poet, the artist in me. When I feel that sense of inspiration, I am transported to the thousands of times I've been in that world. I can feel the joy of the world slowing down my focus so I am more present. I can feel the change in my energy, the tantalizing expression beckoning me forward into whatever unknown essence that is on the brink of revealing itself to me. I am being directed to a new vantage point. And this vantage point always holds the element of surprise, the delight that opens petal after petal of a cosmic flowering kind of experience that moves in the breeze of a moment and yet guides me on a new journey.

As a visionary life coach, intuitive, and spiritual teacher I am fully open to spirit, to the divine revelation. I am present to inspiration. I have an entire repertoire of inspirational experiences. I invite inspiration into my life, and I can see it everywhere. I see and know the frequencies of that ever-changing energy of wonder and revelation.

For me, traveling and exploring the inter-dimensional universe is a very creative process. I have a unique way of looking at the world, at looking at words, qualities, ways of being and thinking, and wondering if how they appear is really how they are—really the truth of their essence.

I am inspired by the ideas and visions that the Divine shares with me. I am inspired and moved by the perspectives and innovations that the Divine will explain to me. I listen for the alchemy. I wait for the ethereal whispers so I can transcend the plain moment and enter the luxury of a mystical present. I love following the magic, and I am an open and willing participant.

Even before I realized my full spiritual and intuitive gifts, I was an artist, a sculptor. That is a profession that pursues inspiration. I would seriously connect with the Divine and listen for the inspiration in my work. At this time in my life I was integrating my powerful intuitive gifts of vision, channeling, and communication with my gifts as an artist, seeing my sculpture fully alive and pulsing with the vision I held. I didn't know I was integrating the two. I was simply, joyfully, and seriously following what vision inspired me and what guidance I heard. To be honest, I was pleasantly relentless.

If you are a visionary or a leader, you wait for inspiration to create community, awareness, relationship, and a greater future. Visionaries have a perspective that rockets into the future and sees possibilities that can improve our lives. Inspiration is the torch, the light, the brilliance you share and the brilliance others joyfully follow. These possibilities are more about relationships and ways of being. You are excited to find new ways that people can communicate, understand each other, and create opportunities for others to develop and fulfill their unique gifts. You value relationship, caring, healing, the well-being of humanity, protection of our natural resources, and a sustainable future for all. You can see ways to improve and elevate relationship and the future of our world. You may provide this vision and leadership in your immediate family, in your children's schools, in your local environment, and as a global activist.

Inspiration means creating a better life. You see the importance of developing strong, honoring, and equal relationships. You want to support the beauty and contribution of all people. You have a strong awareness of the planet-wide issues: education, community, personal development, spiritual growth, and evolution and support of good causes that benefit everyone, not a select few. This may bring you to leadership and volunteer positions in your school, your associations, your community, your business, or in any area that you feel you can make a contribution.

Chapter 3:

The ART of Living Inspired

The ART of Living Inspired is a blessing from Divine Source and an opportunity for personal participation. Inspiration is Awakening, Revelation, and Transformation. So, what is it about inspiration that makes us yearn for it? Why is it so desirable? Why do so many people hunger to be touched by this magic?

Inspiration happens in many ways and circumstances. Inspiration is a profound moment when magic enters your life and whispers, sings, or shouts a true divine message of transformation to you. This moment is for you and you alone. This is a kiss, an embrace of synchronicity that transports you to a new and brilliant thought, expression, realization, and future.

You want to be inspired. You want to be lifted beyond what you know into something beautiful, magical, and filled with possibility. You want to have a direct experience of the Divine, in which you are moved into a greater recognition and feel embraced and acknowledged. It is thrilling.

Naturally, there are all levels of experience. Sometimes inspiration can be subtle. Sometimes it can be boldly profound. No matter what, the world stops. Time halts for a moment and you are flooded by whatever idea, image, connection, wisdom, or expression reveals itself to you.

In each aspect of your personal experience of inspiration, the vibrational steps of awareness and activation usually follow the pattern described in the following sections.

Awakening

You become conscious of a new energy that captures your attention and focus. Now you see the light. You don't know what the light is yet, but you see it. The first aspect of inspiration is the awakening.

Inspiration will grab your attention. It is light streaming into a prism of your mind and capturing the rainbow. All of these colors shift your attention and focus. All you can see are these sparking rainbows that vitalize you.

You are becoming alert to something out of the ordinary. There is energy here. Sometimes you will get goose bumps and chills. Sometimes you will feel absolutely riveted and it feels like the world stands still. Sometimes it's deeply quiet, and in this stillness, you feel like you are going inward to discover a magical treasure and all of your attention is focused in one moment.

Awakening is the "Ah Ha!" It is the surprise. It feels like somebody tapped you on the shoulder, and when you turn around, the familiar becomes brighter, more colorful, and more important.

When I was a sculptor, I really would watch for this

part, because once this was engaged, I knew the rest of the inspiration was going to blast forward. I would wait for the blurry, fuzzy feeling that I got just before the full energy of inspiration would captivate me.

I worked in clay and mixed media, creating large installation and environmental pieces. I was always inspired in some way. I listened for it. I was poised for every moment of inspiration that would come and direct my spirit, my mind, or my hands.

This usually translated into a new piece, whether I was making a single large piece for a gallery show or creating a multi-piece installation for an outdoor site. I would see into the future of the piece and experience soundless direction. I worked for hours straight. Sculpture in clay is physical. I moved, pushed, pounded, and draped all while circling the piece to see it from every angle. I always entered the zone, the space in mind and spirit where only the sculpture existed and I was simply there to make it happen. It may have looked like action, but it always had a center of calm awareness and joy.

I can give you an example of the night my whole way of working changed. I was working in clay, sculpting faces and body parts. They were going to be suspended from the ceiling of the museum gallery so you would walk through them. I had probably 33 pieces all lined up, draped on several worktables around my loft space.

I was laughing, smiling, and in action. Then I felt the pause and tingle. I know this feeling, because for me, that's the inspiration buzz. Everything slows down, almost stops in silence, and then I have a slight tingle. Sometimes it will be outright goose bumps, sometimes just a buzz.

This instance I felt the buzz. I stopped. When inspiration comes, stop. You have to be present for it. You can't ignore it or you will lose the moment. I stopped, with tools in one hand and rolling pin in another. And I listened. That's what I always do when inspiration comes calling.

I listen. For some inexplicable reason I heard, "Smash them." I started to laugh. Really? Weeks' worth of work for a museum show? Smash them?

You know I did. I smooshed them, pushed them, and moved the faces, arms, and body parts into forms of sculpture that looked distorted and yet free. I rolled over some of them with my rolling pin. This was not what I had originally envisioned.

This piece was a turning point in my career and a huge breakthrough in my work. Once I agreed and really listened to my inspiration, I had so much fun. My creativity and voice was liberated, and so were the pieces. They became more like falling leaves than body parts.

The curator of the museum loved them. The art critics loved them, and I reached a new dimension in my art.

Inspiration's energy of awakening is like the music in film. The music in the film actually predicts the mood and precedes the event. If it's going to be a romantic scene, the string sections or flutes start up before the event. If you are watching an action film, the dramatic music starts several moments before the action takes place, heightening your awareness and anticipation for the car chases to come. With inspiration's awakening, you can feel the slight anticipation. It's getting exciting. It's joyful and wondrous, and you know there is something coming, but it's still unknown. You just know it's going to be good.

Awakening brings you the moments of anticipation and awareness. Something good is coming. Pay attention. Something good is coming. Get ready.

Revelation

You are activated, you are stimulated, and you come alive in this moment to perceive something new and wonderful. The universe discloses something to you. Life announces, discloses, explains, and imparts something special to you.

However you see this, whether you experience it as a profound thought that leads you to a new opening, feel it as a divine proclamation that calls you to attention, or hear it as a symphony of synchronicity that aligns to make sure you notice it all, the universe is revealing something to you and you must take notice. This is a vision, idea, understanding, or expression that comes to you personally.

Inspiration happens to you. You are being acted upon. You are being called. You are being triggered. You are being shown something new. Inspiration is communicating with you in a very specific, personal way to show you something unique and different in a manner that will capture your attention and imagination.

You are personally engaged in this event. It involves you and it affects you. You know something more. You see something unique. Pieces fall together in new and unimagined ways. The light goes on and you can see, know, feel, sense, and realize something profound and rich.

Not only is inspiration an "Ah Ha!" moment, it is a "Ta Da!" moment. The universe is saying "Ta Da! Look behind the curtain into the miraculous. I wave my wand and you can see the magic. Look at this wonderful, special aspect of reality and see! This is for you."

Revelation brings you into the moment. Have you ever been to the ocean? Imagine that you are driving up a winding road with sand dunes on either side. You can smell the salt air. You can feel the ocean breeze, but the ocean is not in view.

You crest the bluff in your car, and right in front of you the panorama of the ocean is revealed in one amazing sweep. Do you remember your first time seeing the ocean? No words can describe what it's like to see that vast blue reaching out to touch the sky at the horizon.

That is revelation.

As you travel inside your inspiration, you are following that road in the sand dunes. You may have a vision of your life as you go forward and then, in the middle of that vision, you see yourself, helping others or creating beauty or talking with other people and standing back to look at something you did not imagine you would do.

In life, it may not look like the vision in your revelation. It will feel like it. The vision or words or meaning is to inspire you, not paint the whole picture. So, when inspiration touches you and guides you, let the panorama captivate you and reveal its magic. This is why you pursue inspiration. It is the wonder of it all.

Transformation

You are altered and changed by this sacred moment. This special encounter shifts you in a profound way. You are altered in some aspect of yourself. Perhaps now you understand something very profound. You feel renewed and revitalized because whatever you realized in the revelation, now you are changed. Now you understand. Now a metamorphosis is taking place within you that guides you in a new way.

Inspiration without transformation is just a good insight. Inspiration without transformation is just a good idea. Inspiration without transformation is just a good method or technique or reorganization of systems and steps. That's exciting, but inspiration requires transformation, and that is a powerful component.

Transformation alters you and brings you to a higher state of being. You are uplifted. Your vision is clearer. You are thinking and functioning at a higher level. This stage of inspiration infuses the revelation and wisdom of your divine message and helps you integrate and change into a higher expression. The transformation that takes place is instant; it also evolves over time.

Your new perspective, your energy shift, influences a different set of decisions. From this place of deeper understanding, with a new understanding of your soul purpose, you create a bigger opening in your life. You feel like you're sharper, smarter, and clearer about life. You may think in more complex terms but achieve success with simple actions and results. It feels like everything is falling into place. Everything makes more sense.

Inspiration changes you. It brings you to a new awareness and then—you are altered. The cells through to your DNA shift to accommodate this brilliant, light-filled experience and vibrationally you shift in your essence, so you can carry the inspiration forward.

In more simple terms, when inspiration first touches you and you let that inspiration in, you receive a new way of thinking, perceiving, or being that alters how you see the world. This is part of the transformation. If you are a musician and inspiration hits, then you hear your song, you feel the music in a new way, and this changes you. When you are an innovator and inspiration touches you, then the old ways of doing things fall into the distance and the new perceptions take over. Then you see and understand things from that framework, and this enlightens and informs everything else you do.

If you've never been inspired, if you've never had this experience—you want it.

If you have had this experience, if you have been inspired—you want it more.

Chapter 4:

Multi-Dimensional Flow

Everything you do has repercussions in the world and beyond. That means that what you do in your life influences all life on our world. Your inspiration changes the world. I personally feel it influences all of consciousness everywhere. I want to explore and illustrate just how that may look when you are Living Inspired.

Here's an example of an exponential approach to Living Inspired, so you can see how the inspiration flows multi-dimensionally:

1. I coach, teach, and write books because that is how I can really make a difference. I pursue and discover and explore those gifts of inspiration at every level possible. This helps my own gifts—my intuitive and visionary gifts—to become even more enhanced and profound. So I am Living Inspired. I am pursuing and captivating my own inspiration. I am active in connecting with the multi-dimensional energy, insights, and wisdom of inspiration. I am also devoted to realizing and sharing

these many layers in my life. Now, Living Inspired, I can accelerate my vision, my purpose, and my destiny.

2.   Then I expand it. My own gifts come forward to create magic, bringing amazing transformations to help you bring your true gifts forward. I recognize the truth illuminated in your soul and purpose. I can see the gifts and the higher version of your lives. I can see the greater aspects that will help you transform into "the *more* of you." I share all of this with you: this book, my private coaching, and my seminars. This expands inspiration from my world into yours. Now you have a greater opportunity to experience inspiration.

3.   Inspiration begins to flow in you. I've helped you ignite the truth illuminated in your soul and purpose. You are taking steps to bring this into your life in new and unexpected ways. This brings your true gifts forward. You are celebrating on a whole new level of your own path.

4.   This inspires me. Now I am inspired, again, by being a catalyst for your inspiration. I become even more acutely aware of the reach of inspiration. I can see that when I actively engage it, when I am at cause and I am the motivator, generator, and initiator, I am creating ripples of inspiration that go beyond what I created inside of me. I have inspired you. You are now open to inspiration in a more expansive way.

In this stage of the evolution of inspiration, you are celebrating a whole new level on your own path and you are open to inspiration in a grander way. Picture your life from this perspective:

- Can you see how this is expanding your view of your own capacities?

- Do you recognize new opportunities that are opening up for you and give you more than you had access to before?

- Whom do you impact and influence with the inspiration that is flowing in you?

- Who are the people in your family who are sensing and responding to your joyful changes?

- Can they feel the shift in you?

- Have you shared this new perspective with colleagues, business associates, and co-workers?

- Have you shared this change, this new perspective with your family and friends?

It doesn't even matter whether your family and friends are excited for you and support you, which of course I hope they do. Just by sharing your own inspiration, you have touched their lives with new possibilities. You are starting to really engage in your vision. That is inspiring to others.

5. Now, I am Living Inspired. You are Living Inspired. Together, our vision, purpose, and destiny have expanded beyond what was originally in place. This is an example of the way the Awakening and Revelation aspects of Living Inspired can occur.

6. The transformation generated through Living Inspired is evident in everything. When people see and understand the difference between being inspired and Living Inspired, they will be able to take their own inspiration, soul purpose, and vision even further. This empowers each of them and helps uplift our world in so many different ways.

   Now, in this example, two people sharing inspiration actively brought inspiration to another level. Then it moves forward to influence many other people.

7. The people in our lives are now experiencing our shift. Your family and friends are seeing new possibilities in their own lives because you are actively pursuing your dreams and inspiration. Now they are intrigued. They are also starting to take their own potential more seriously. Your family and friends, colleagues, business associates, and co-workers are receiving waves of inspiration from you. They can see their own dreams and potential. They feel there is more to their lives, and they are ready to explore and take action, too.

8. At this point, all of us reverberate in so many different ways and the inspiration, gifts, unique perspectives, and wisdom are now far-reaching. So many more

people are blessing the world with their inspiration and gifts. It grows from there.

This creates an expanding circle of influence. Living Inspired has grown exponentially. So many things have evolved. Each aspect has a positive life of its own.

Thousands of people are touched and elevated. The shared personal vision and experience inspires others to connect with their own gifts and deeper purpose. This ripples out into the world in waves of conscious connection from the individual, then to a personal circle, then to an expanding circle of people and beyond.

Family, friends, co-workers, associates, and their circles of influence stretch beyond the people we can count and name. It stretches beyond familiar boundaries. The influence of our collective inspiration is truly global. We are now causing a global shift and we are an active, integral part of that change.

9. In this moment, in this realization, we are Living Inspired. We are seeing and living within the positive changes that Living Inspired generated. In the joy of that, we are going to expand even further. We are going to see our purpose and destiny in a greater light. We are now an active part of the mystery, and it continues.

Focus on the changes you make, not on the actions you take. The effects and reverberation of your Living Inspired and my Living Inspired change the world. We haven't even taken any actions yet.

Looking Forward

In the first section I revealed a unique and extraordinary life of inspiration and how it moves you. Hundreds of millions of people are seeking inspiration. As you already know from reading this far, I'm not giving you simple suggestions to get inspired. This is not a book about taking a walk in nature or letting go of the things that distract you. While those are perfect suggestions and they can help, this book has a bigger vision. First, this is a big, bold exploration of what inspiration really is and which preconceived notions block you from your passion and your path.

For example, one preconceived notion that blocks you from your passion and your path, even if it's subliminal, is the thought or fear that inspiration can take hold of you in a bad way. There is nothing to worry about if you are inspired. That's all Hollywood movie stuff. You are not going to sit drooling and incoherently ranting about things. Do not be worried or concerned about being captured by feeling driven. You are not going to forsake your family and friends and start a crusade. Of course, if you are already doing that, it isn't inspiration. Let's just say that's part of your charm.

Who do you think of when you think of an inspired leader or visionary? Do you think of Steve Jobs? Do you think of Martin Luther King? Do you think of Oprah? Do you think of Princess Diana?

Inspiration grants you the insight to see deeper, to explore your own dreams, to create new dreams if you don't have them, to feel a deep connection to something greater than yourself, and to share that with others. Inspiration is an infusion of wisdom and clarity. It brings real qualities into your life or supports the qualities and dreams you already have so you can be "the more of you." This book helps you discover how you can actively experience and live in the essence and qualities of inspiration.

So What Are Those Qualities?

In the next section, I'm going to explore the different qualities, aspects, and energies of inspiration. When you know the qualities, you can actively engage them. This is much better, more efficient, and more lasting than a great to-do list telling you what to eliminate in your life so you can be inspired. These are the qualities, frequencies, and rich energies that generate inspiration.

Remember the banquet I mentioned earlier? I told you that to be open to inspiration, you create your own banquet. I suggested that you be open and nonjudgmental to ideas or thoughts that show up.

I've prepared a vibrational banquet for you. All of these qualities, attributes, and energies are your guests. Enjoy the personality of each aspect. Entertain them. Dance with them. Listen to their stories. You don't have to marry them, but if you ignore or judge them before you even let them sing their own songs, then you are interrupting the flow of inspired music and possibilities in your life.

Please join this banquet. Bon appétit!

The Sacred Story:

Oceans of Time

Early morning on the beach in autumn was a secret time. The beach was hers alone. It was deserted.

Maya wore a heavy coat and wrapped her cashmere scarf around her neck. The wind was cold, the ocean looked like ice, and it was magic.

She sat, took her journal from her bag, and grabbed her large cappuccino. The biscotti were still in the bag, but that could wait. She loved the quiet. It was a luxury, even though most people would physically and literally shudder at the whipping wind and white-capped waves. To her this was paradise.

Her life was completely engulfed by things that once seemed so important and now seemed insignificant. Being alone, feeling the strong wind blow by the sea, was meditation. She took another sip of the coffee and stared at the waves.

There will be time. She took a deep breath and grabbed her pen to write random thoughts, streams of consciousness. She didn't write anything important. Just words, phrases, and scribbles. It was her own secret code of nothingness to free her mind and heart.

"I am here and I am listening..." She smiled and closed her eyes.

A shadow crossed over her chair. She heard faint laughter and opened her eyes.

He wasn't visible, silhouetted by the sun low on the horizon, but she could feel him smile.

"It's time," he said. His voice was deep, but easy.

"Excuse me?"

"It's time," he said. Then he nodded his head.

"I'm not following."

"It's time to go. You are not following. You are leading. It's time." He laughed a warmhearted laugh.

At the same time, a flock of seagulls swooped low, creating a racket. Maya looked up to see the birds and laughed. She returned her gaze, adjusting to the light, and he was gone. She looked around for a sign that she had even seen this man, but there was no hint—no shadow, no footsteps.

She touched her journal. Neatly written in someone else's hand, "I am here and I am listening. It's time to go. You are not following. You are leading. It's time."

She smiled. Light streamed into awareness. NOW.

PART 2:

Follow the Light

The Answer Is Yes

One moment captures many heartbeats
Hummingbirds scatter buzzing the air in search of nectar
Light spattered in patterns of love running across
the grass   laughing.
She just stared
The world was opening

Move into the brilliance
Stand in the light
Breathe
She stepped in
Exultation
Illumination

She swooned in joy
The light echoed her names and her dreams
She said yes.
The answer is always yes.

Chapter 5:

Vibrating into the Tri-Light

The divine messages of inspiration want to find you. These expressions of sacred connection are created specifically for you, in harmony with your personal resonance, soul purpose, unique gifts, and destiny. While the experience can move from a soft whisper of awareness to a dazzling shift in perspective, each opening communication is of light.

The overall light frequency of inspiration blends together into the Tri-Light, a threefold energy dynamic of ART—Awakening, Revelation, and Transformation.

> **AWAKENING** captures your attention. Light streams into the prism of your mind, heart, and being.

> **REVELATION** announces, discloses, reveals, and imparts. Now you see the light! You recognize something that was once hidden. You see more clearly, and it moves you.

TRANSFORMATION encourages change. You are altered and changed by this light-filled sacred moment. A metamorphosis is taking place. The cells through to your DNA shift to accommodate this brilliant, light-filled transformation. The light changes you. Now you understand.

When the ART of Living Inspired happens, the highest frequencies come into play. You receive an infusion. Your whole system—meaning your physical body, your mind, your awareness, your soul, and your emotions—all experience a light-filled shift.

You feel a rush. This is an energy swoop. It swoops in and enlightens you. You have feelings of greater awareness and sometimes of exultation. The reason I'm describing all of this is because if you are shopping for inspiration, you want to know your size and whether the store carries that piece.

If you are pursuing inspiration and want to Live Inspired, it's advantageous to know how inspiration shows up and how it feels. You want to know it. Then you can distinguish it, relish it, and be open to its enlightening transformative powers.

Inspiration is a happy, positive feeling and energy. Each experience of inspiration can be distinct and diverse. You can experience the frequencies of inspiration for a brief moment or for days. It's not unusual for people to just start to laugh about their experience, laugh in the energy of it hours or days afterward. It's all good. It's all welcome. It's all inspirational.

The Tri-Light is the three major light expressions of the frequencies of inspiration. They are the most distinguished ways of knowing how inspiration may appear, influence, and affect you.

The Sweet Light

The Sweet Light experience of inspiration is joy, elation, wonder, beauty, and delight.

You experience gladness and even giddiness. You will feel buoyant, optimistic, and happy. You can feel the energy move, and it energizes you to take notice. The feelings usually coincide with the inspiration, but sometimes they can come before, during, or after.

You have just experienced the Sweet Light of inspiration.

You are a songwriter and musician, and you've been doing this for a while. In the songwriting process, you opened up to a new inspiration. In that moment, some of the lyrics you wrote in the past are coming back to you in a new way. They mean something bigger, with more nuances than you imagined when you wrote them and sang them years ago. You feel that sweet flash and light chills that you get when inspiration is present.

This triggers a new spark. It's sweet. You can see the connection from your past weaving into you right here in this moment of creation. You can feel the relevance today of the words in your past. It makes you delighted. How wonderful the connections from the past brought you here today; there is a theme, a relationship that ties your life together.

You are a healer. Your work with other people brings them clearing, healing, and greater health. As you consider several of your clients, you feel and sense new thoughts coming into place. There is a new connection and synthesis that is weaving patterns together in a new way. It's bringing new meaning and methods to you.

You are feeling a slight tingling right now that lets you know something magical is happening. Inspiration is pouring in. You keep feeling light and joy and intrigue. The light of that inspired moment is calling you and directing you to experience more of that wisdom.

We are all here to give voice to our lives and our dreams. Each passage, each chapter of your life, brings a wisdom that carries your voice into the universe. A clear vision always brings your heart and your truth into expression.

The Divine calls you, calls all of us into existence. Inspiration is the universe's invitation to you, to participate and join in the universe's grand design. The Sweet Light of inspiration calls to you and pulls you into that light.

Inspiration invites you, including you in the magic and mystery of that creation. This is intimate. The universe calls to you, so you can amplify your creations and shine a sweet light back to her.

The Sweet Light of inspiration acknowledges you as a writer of your own story. When inspiration touches you, it invites you, with your gifts, wisdom, and heart to share in the creation of new visions, a new story that you are invited to write. The Sweet Light of inspiration is your invitation to light the way. Are you ready to bring your light into the world?

The Beaming Light

The Beaming Light experience of inspiration is a "rock your world" experience.

You will feel exultation, euphoria, ecstasy, paradise, rapture, and jubilance. This makes the experience feel more significant. It is powerful and often visceral. You usually don't ignore this one. You are moved. You may get chills. You may be moved to tears. You may be moved to dance. The effects of this inspiration can last for days and weeks. You may even shake your head or burst into tears weeks later because the echoes of this wisdom still move you deeply. You may feel motivated to share—immediately. It's not unusual to hear a lot of "Oh! Wow!"

You are experiencing the Beaming Light of inspiration.

The world just shook. You had an amazing, far-reaching insight into your whole business. Everything is moving very quickly in you. You are regrouping, meaning your mind is trying to slow down the input, but at the same time, you know you have to run with it. You'll make more sense out of it later. Every time you think about this, you get chills. This is it! This is it! Everything makes sense.

You are in business and have been working to integrate several pieces of your business and you were making progress, but it just didn't seem right.

Suddenly, a big flash of something happened and you could see how this piece of the business was actually in the way of your success. Well, if you sold that, if you changed the perspective and focused on another piece.... Okay, this is going to be amazing. This changes everything. You can see where you were stuck and you don't even care.

That's over. This is so good.

Immediately, you feel like the world has shifted. You know this is a powerful moment that you will remember as your turning point. You never thought of your life in this way. You didn't realize the depth of possibility or the shifts you could make or the real influence this will have in your life and in the world.

Maybe the Beaming Light of inspiration has nothing to do with your business and everything to do with helping, or healing, or reaching out to a community in need. You know you are ready. You are ready right now. You didn't see this before, or maybe you just didn't believe you could do this. Now you know you can. Now the joy in your heart and the beauty of your soul join together and you see exactly what you need to do to make a difference. This is really what lights you up.

Now, you are pacing. You are walking around the room and talking with your hands. No, you have to write this down. No, you have to let it fly. No, you need a coffee. No, you need to call someone. No, you need to sit down and write this. Yes. That's good. Write this down. You feel the joy, the power of the inspiration and it is rocking your world. The Beaming Light opened up a new world.

You see your vision.

Three weeks later, you have copious notes. You are still completely jazzed. It's even bigger. The inspiration keeps on growing and you are part of it. It's not just happening to you, you are inside it and it is inside you. Okay, maybe you can't explain it, but you feel it. It is so much bigger than you thought. "Oh! Wow!"

The Brilliant Light

The Brilliant Light experience of inspiration is deeper or more delightfully subtle.

You will feel luxury, gratitude, awe, deep peace, and silence, exhilaration, and celebration. You may feel a sense of fulfillment and deepening, without a specific reason for feeling that depth. The brilliant light experience fills you in a deeper way. Usually this experience is the most challenging to describe and share. The intimacy and awareness of this infusion can bring a quiet, enlightening realization. You may never be able to describe it in words, but the power and consciousness is there.

You are experiencing the Brilliant Light of inspiration.

Deep and powerful thoughts and energies are moving. You feel supreme gratitude. You are really paying attention to the voice, the instrument of inspiration moving through you. You know this is a very important moment—is this a moment, or have you been in this inspired state for hours? Don't know. Don't care. It is encompassing. Your reality is shifting and changing and it is beautiful.

There is something very quiet, very deep, and very right about this. You may not be sure how this fits in, but you know it will. Maybe it relates to your business, but it seems bigger. Not sure.

Oh. Right now, it's not about how it fits in or what you do. It's more important to be present. You can feel an infusion of energy and wisdom and insight that amazes and delights you. This is fast, but it feels slow, like time is slowing down so you can understand this and then bring it into your life.

This may not be an idea. This may not translate into your business, your art, or your family. This may be a view of the world that has to unfold over time. And guess what? You really feel like you can savor this. You couldn't describe it yet, anyway, but you will, in time. Right now, it is deep and you are quietly exhilarated.

You know a month from now, this will still move you. This could be a new way of life. It feels that important. Right now, even that doesn't matter. You have to stop thinking and let this inspired ride continue.

Celebrating the Tri-Light

The Sweet Light, the Brilliant Light and the Beaming Light express the frequencies of inspiration in different ways. There are different tones, feelings, and intensities of these light vibrations. I've described them so you can distinguish their differences and not discount the more quiet energies while you wait for that blast of inspiration that brings you to your knees. The intensity of the message itself is not always indicative of the intensity of the revelation. It's simply how you respond to the inspiration, the message, and the light streaming your way. What one person may experience as earth-shattering, another may experience as a sweet whisper. It's similar to how we respond to a lot of things. One joke may make you chuckle while your friend is absolutely hysterical with laughter.

When you want to Live Inspired, these three different rays of light will alert you to the experience that inspiration brings. When you have a greater understanding of the radiance of each ray, then you can be receptive to the divine message. You will see it, know it, feel it, perceive it, and be open to it. This is active participation. When you know the signals and indications of these three rays of light, you can consciously invite them into your being. You can be joyfully vigilant to the divine call. Now you are present.

Chapter 6:

Entering the Seven Temples of Vibrating Light

Welcome to the Seven Temples of Vibrating Light. The seven temples of vibrating light hold the vibrational spaces and celestial attunements so you can experience the gifts of Inspiration. Each temple has a unique resonance that reveals a special gift. Each temple also attunes you in different ways.

Please remove your shoes and bow your head as you enter and greet the Priestess. The divine gifts await you. Blessings are bestowed upon those who enter with honor, joy, and appreciation.

Now each brilliant connection of inspiration, each of these seven temples of vibrating light, can interact with you. If your own life path is in harmony and your soul purpose and destiny is in the higher octave of alignment, then you may be able to enter each and every temple to expand your connection to the gifts of inspiration that you carry. Otherwise, you will favor certain temples that are more compatible with your purpose and path.

The seven temples of vibrating light are the active ingredients that kindle new life into inspiration so it lives on in new and wondrous ways. When you can distinguish these individual and separate frequencies, you will understand the nuances of energy that create inspiration. Through Awakening, Revelation, and Transformation, the three stages of the ART of inspiration, new vibrational attributes continue to create greater divine collaborative expression.

Inspiration itself creates something new. When inspiration touches you, then you become a new component of the vibration of inspiration. You, as the beneficiary of the vibration, create another layer of expression with the source of inspiration. Out of this combination comes something more. You are different in a profound, life-altering way. This personal metamorphosis brings you to a new brilliance. You can carry the brilliance forward in a way that is vibrant, meaningful, creative, and transformational, not only for yourself, but also for the world.

Just watching, being able to see the magnificence of everything shining its own masterful proficiency, always impresses me. It is an honor to witness this brilliant complexity in action. The Divine artfully weaves the threads of existence together. I still am in joyful awe and appreciation seeing the different aspects of one seemingly wondrous and simple experience, like inspiration revealed in its profound complexity. To behold this divine revelation and experience the shift in your being, is to behold the mysteries. It is resplendent. You become part of the secret.

My personal understanding, truth, and knowing is that *inspiration creates the universe.* The Divine is not simply a creation mechanism, lavishly sending out new creations just because She can and it's part of what She does. The Divine creates with inspiration. She is inspired by a brilliance, a greater knowing than we can comprehend, and then She presents that astonishing gift to us. Whatever the creation is, whether we can even perceive the essence of that creation, it is inspired into being. We, if we are aware, are the recipients of that magnanimous treasure.

Even when you are Being Inspired, the treasure is priceless. I just thought you should know.

When you are part of the vibrations of inspiration, you are Living Inspired. The more you can savor the brilliance of the universe, the more you can understand the ways and wisdom of inspiration, the more it shows up in your life. Living Inspired is participatory! You have to play in it. That is what this is about. To wake up and realize the brilliance of the universe is contacting you, by way of inspiration. Now you can contact the universe back.

When the Divine, the Goddess, the Universe brings you inspiration, this means you are singled out, you are selected to receive. You are being called. You can feel honored. You can feel moved. You can simply feel happy that you have a seat at the banquet.

You can be a participant in the miraculous. Say "Thank you!"

Inspiration, messages, transformations, and light let you know that you are a real part of creation. The Ultimate Consciousness, the Creatrix of All has truly focused on you. She is revealing wisdom to you, including you in a sweet secret, sharing something beautiful, moving, uplifting, and precious.

Say "Thank you" and then pay rapt attention, with respect and honor. This does not happen to you every day.

Remember, if there is no ART, if there is no Awakening, Revelation, and Transformation, then it's all just a great idea. You want to Live Inspired. Then your inspiration is more than a great idea. It can guide you to a greater part of yourself and help you shine in whatever you do. You can gain a richer understanding of true brilliance.

I will now introduce you to the Seven Temples of Vibrating Light.

Chapter 7:

Temple 1 ~
The Illumination

As you enter The Illumination, inspiration brings you light and energy. This light energy is the first impulse, the first notice, and the first indication of your inspiration. Light-filled spirit "highlights" you and prepares you to receive the magic energies. It creates an inner glow.

The universe is shining a light within you so you can benefit and shine. Inspiration is the experience of the universe, the Divine, singling you out to share something awe-inspiring.

This Illumination changes and modulates because of who you are. The light matrix emphasizes your experience, and brings attention to what is happening in your awakening and revelation. It imparts light so you can fully recognize the importance of the moment. In this light-filled eternal moment, the Illumination is the signal for you to recognize that something life-altering is happening.

Light quickens. It is enlightening. Its luminous quality informs you that there is more to this experience, more to this shared brilliance than just a great idea or impulse.

It is an agent of change. It is part of your transformation. This way of revealing itself, of the divine message and impression shining into you, allows and encourages you to see what is happening and then use this light to grow, to awaken, to move beyond your limitations. It is a life-altering event. It brings light to the situation and then everyone who is astute and aware can perceive the genius of your experience and the wisdom you received.

Think of light speed. Think of spotlight. With that light, and in harmony with the wisdom of the inspiration you received or generated, you can step out into the spotlight. When you are in harmony with the inspiration, then those people who are in harmony with you can see the wisdom you received. You are also illuminated.

This is a great benefit for you in your soul and in your life. This is a great benefit for you sharing your inspiration in the world. Think of your inspiration as a positive light shining for those who are ready for a more brilliant path.

Ask Yourself:

What light-filled actions can I take to grow and move beyond my limitations?

How can I share my inspiration and bring my positive light into the world?

How can I share my inspiration and begin Living Inspired to illuminate and support the people and businesses working for the greater good in our world?

Chapter 8:

Temple 2 ~
The Magnetism

The Magnetism attracts your attention and pulls your focus to whatever it lights up. It grabs you. It pulls people toward you. It also captures other people so that like-minded people will join you. It calls forth more energy, more ideas, and more of your attention.

This attraction, interest, and allure begin with you. The message of the inspiration is attracted to you because of your soul purpose, your spiritual journey, and your life experience. Your own soul calls and enthralls the attention of the Divine. You are now part of this magnetic attraction, the vortex of cosmic interest.

Now you are magnetic and you are attracting the circumstances to fulfill the inspiration you received. The Magnetism attracts great things. This positive attraction brings kindred essences together. This helps you fulfill the pathways created by inspiration.

The Magnetism can become a guidance system for others to find you and help fulfill the dreams of the universe that were shared with you. This is a great benefit for you, especially if you are inspired to be entrepreneurial or create a business to attract other people to see you, join you, and support you. Your business, whether you are just starting out or already established, always benefits from positive attention and growth. Being able to attract those people and circumstances that see and know the benefits of what you provide, is a great help all the way around.

When you are generating business from an inspired place, when your vision goes beyond providing products and services and reflects your own inspiration and the gifts the universe shares with you, then others who can see and feel this will know the connection they have with you. They will be attracted to your business.

Why were you attracted to this book? We have a shared connection. The message, subject, or resonance of this book called to you in some way, and now you are reading it. Your soul purpose, destiny, spiritual journey, and life call you to experience more about inspiration. This specific book is in your hands for a very important reason. This book and the energies within it will bring you closer to your own path.

The Magnetism attracted you to this book to fulfill something for you. This positive attraction guided you to the meaning, message, and teachings of this book for reasons that may be known to you, or may be quickly revealed.

Think of your inspiration as a positive, spiritual magnet. You will still have products and provide services, and the people who are astute, who can allow a bigger guidance to attract their attention and loyalty, will find you. They will be attracted to the wisdom you received. You are also magnetic.

Ask Yourself:

What attracts my attention and guides my vision to share my gifts and fulfill my soul purpose?

What actions can I take to attract greater fulfillment, inspiration and purpose in my life?

How can I begin Living Inspired so that we all attract better products, more business, and more clients who work for the greater good in our world?

Chapter 9:

Temple 3 ~ The Reverberation

I n one moment, you are quickened by inspiration. The Reverberation sends harmonic resonance into the world. This is a toning and a song that begins with the Divine and embraces you. Your heartstrings echo your soul purpose and this creates symphonic waves through you and the world. You are in the midst of a ripple effect. These energies vibrate together, complementing the sound and music of spirit. They move outward. They begin to tune like with like. Your heartstrings resonate in a similar way to plucking a guitar string in a room of other stringed instruments. When you pluck one string, all other strings begin to resonate to that same note.

The temple of energy does the same. Now the joy and awakening of that song, your duet with the Divine, vibrates and begins a chain of connections to the song. Your song moves from you in ripples, attuning other ripples and echoing your inspiration.

The Reverberation helps you carry the inspiration forward, to share your vision and generate the fulfillment of that inspiration. Then your soul can reverberate with the genuine quality and harmony of this wonder. When this happens, when you hold the vibration of your genuine inspiration, you broadcast a new harmony.

Those beings who are compatible, who have an affinity to your particular message of inspiration, begin to align and come together. They are attuned to the melody of this unique compatibility of soul and spirit. Your vibration calls people and circumstances to sing that same song. They are now called to share this beauty, harmony, and vision with you. Imagine all of the people sensing this echoing reflection of your inspiration. It goes out into the universe and then reflects back. The energy builds and calls people and energy to the song of your inspiration.

A beautiful theme captures the attention of those souls who are called to this expression. This is a benefit for you, and it sometimes calls for a bigger platform for your inspiration. Your unique experience now echoes in song and becomes a symphony, inviting those who love this music to join and play. Your experience and encounter may feel personal and private. It is often more than a personal vision. It reaches beyond your individuality. The reverberations of this gift, of this inspiration, are that you can bless and move thousands and millions of people in the same moment. The way this energy moves through you and then outward into the hearts of many generates a realm of harmonic wonder. Isn't this what the Divine does with us?

There have been national and global moments of peace, when one inspired person initiated a movement to call attention to peace. That person shared their inspired vision with others. This vision reverberated within each person who was called to join forces. Soon groups of people shared that inspiration. Each person was touched, was moved to action through the reverberation as it flowed through that one person, and then as it flowed through everyone. Soon millions of people meditated, prayed, and sent thoughts and visions of peace throughout the world on that date and time. Our world was saturated with good will, blessings, and energies of peace.

The Reverberation calls us out to play. It calls each person individually and plays our heartstrings. Then, all heartstrings play a symphony together. We expand. We come together. Each with our own vision, together in harmony. Inspiration reverberates; it echoes through the dimensions. You can participate in the sacred vibration and call others and invite them to play in the brilliance and wonder of the All.

Ask Yourself:

What vision and wisdom is reverberating in me that calls my gifts forward?

What inspired action or thought is calling to me that I can put in place for the greater good in our world?

No matter how global, local, or situational, see how you can play a role in sharing the magic that happens when inspiration reverberates.

Chapter 10:

Temple 4 ~
The Connection

L ight filaments woven in magic and time hold you in the treads of the Connection to the source of the All, which is the source of your inspiration. The Connection joins you to the elegant universal flow of kinship, relationship, and affinity. You enter the essence of Divine Source. The embrace of higher truth and harmony emblazons your individual soul purpose, intertwining your destiny with the movement of planets and futures that all relate to each other. When the light of inspiration touches you, it connects us all. Your vision inspires our vision. Your light connects us to all light. We may not directly share the same experience, but I see and know the similarity in you.

This aspect of inspiration creates invisible light tendrils that gently connect people, places, ideas, and feelings. The associations that take place in the etheric world translate and affect our natural world. We are connected by the similarities of our experiences and soul purpose.

You are a messenger of divine inspiration. This connects you to the Divine, because you received the ART of inspiration. This connects you to everything and to each of us, because that is the nature of spirit. Your inspiration becomes a spiral of inclusion.

The feeling and knowing that you are connected is extremely important. You know you are not alone and you know that you are part of something bigger and greater than your own world.

The Connection embraces you in the sacred tapestry, through which your inspiration inspires others who are enfolded in this light.

How it may manifest is that people feel connected to you by what you share and what you have received as message, light, and change within yourself. This can definitely help you connect with people who share your vision, who are inspired by your inspiration, and who see in you what you may not even see in yourself. You can benefit from the connections with other people and other systems. You can establish relationships with people who are like-minded and want to feel that connection with others. This creates a sense of unity, a feeling and a knowing that we are all one. Whether you feel connected to me personally, you had the guidance to connect with this energy and material. You may feel something very tangible in my words and want to connect on a deeper level through my workshops or coaching programs. You may connect with this book because you know other people who would benefit from this guidance and wisdom. The connection you feel is a resonance, a tangible energy that you can use for guidance.

Think about the power and importance of this kind of guidance. Think about the actions you could take, and the decisions you could make if you were aware of and engaging with the Connection. The connections you make can lead to greater things—more success, more joy, and more fulfillment for you and for those in your ever-expanding circle.

In business, you can allow and encourage a true sense of connection with your clients. I have clients that I feel deeply connected to and who feel the same way about me. We have a connection that is formed through the trust and wisdom of our inspired visions and by our actions of integrity. These connections, these links to different levels of friendship, business, and wisdom are guided by intuition, inspiration, and good sense. We also sense the "great connector"—the Divine hand—in creating the world wherein nothing is separate.

Ask Yourself:

How am I positively connected to my work, my family, my clients, my business, and the world?

In what ways can I forge a greater sense of connection and relatedness?

Chapter 11:

Temple 5 ~
The Creation

Awakening from the fog of your old dreams, you see the infusion of colors, moments, and prisms of light waiting for the perfect combination of joy and wonder. The Creation embodies the brilliance of all that has been and all that waits for expression in beauty, in grace, and in exuberance. This is the play of energies and possibilities. The fusion, creation, interpretation, reformulation, and new perspectives come fully alive with inspiration. With Inspiration everything is attuned to a positive vision, a valuable and worthy endeavor leading towards a beneficial result.

The Creation generates ideas. It opens the flow of new energy. It encourages you to think and put together new ideas, new thoughts. This fuses the visionary with the innovator and adds the artist and creator. The universe itself comes from this vibrational brilliance.

Now you've got it. Your vision is mixing original new ways of being with known essences to create something new.

Your inspiration may be creating many new things, ideas, opportunities, and capacities for growth, revolution, and change.

Creation causes something to come into being that would not normally evolve on its own. It is at cause, meaning it is the active agent that evokes, motivates and generates. Inspiration—the Awakening, Revelation and Transformation—is causing something that would not have simply evolved, that would not have naturally grown out of those ordinary processes or circumstances. The Divine is the ultimate creator and inspiration.

This is innovation. It initiates, actualizes and brings something new into being. This is the play of energies and possibilities that evoke different relationships, systems and associations. Something new, original, magical and influential is born.

I know it's no surprise to you that I love this part. The creativity of the All, the blessings created and bestowed through originality, imagination, and art just get me soaring. Even if many people's ideas and visions have a similar ring to them, you can create a unique expression that is truly your own. Your innovation can change the world because of who you are, how you perceive the world, and what path your soul chooses to dance.

The Creation flows through everything. You can benefit from the creativity to serve your inspiration and brainstorm the many ways this can show up. Once you do, then you can follow your inspiration and see which path, which creative gateway is the one that shines for you.

There is so much creativity. What creativity, what new inspired inventions and innovations are you bringing out into the world? Sometimes the inspiration is stronger than your focus. This may sound like a challenge; being inspired, you can make it an opportunity. Focus on your inspiration and then open to creative thinking to gather new ideas that will support your vision.

Being in pure creation, you can gather trusted, like-minded friends and colleagues to join in your inspiration and see what creative choices they make to help you grow. You can have an inspiration party. Invite your friends and share in this expanding power, brilliance, and meaning. Let them know what is going on, how moved you are by your inspiration, and then ask them to play along. You are inviting them on the creative journey of your inspiration. Then they can share your inspiration and then share their own inspiration with you.

The creative spark is in everything. Out of seemingly empty space, the world is created. Out of the thoughts and inspiration you receive, you create worlds.

I mean *create*. Create from the inspiration of your soul. This may embolden you to create a business. Inspiration does not give you an outline or provide a "build-by-numbers" format with rules that were handed down by generations of people.

Inspiration encourages you to explore, discover, and follow the dreams that were sparked in that divine communication. The result is that you have a business that is inspired by your vision and functions perfectly in the world.

The Creation is more than brainstorming because the energy, the quality, and the buzz of the inspiration guides the enthusiasm, fueled by transformation and new possibility. You are sharing your personal inspiration. You are also opening those floodgates and encouraging others to play. Once they step into the world that you open to them, they can seize the moment to share your inspiration and fuel it, too.

Maybe your inspiration reveals that you help others gain new perspective and enrichment in their lives. Your inspired creativity can view this as a counseling and healing practice. Your inspired creativity could see this service as a gallery featuring new visions and helping artists successfully bring their ideas into the world. Your inspired creativity could be starting a hot air balloon ride business, giving clients a new perspective in their lives by taking them on a journey to soar above it all.

Ask Yourself:

How can I use the creative flow of inspiration to expand and support my work, my family, my clients, and my business? How can I work with the creative flow of inspiration to personally contribute to the world?

When I know that *inspiration is creative*, where does the flow reveal itself to me and how do I expand on that?

What can I do to help open the floodgates for creativity and new perspectives?

Chapter 12:

Temple 6 ~
The Generosity

The sun rises over oceans of expansion. Light surges across the waves and it opens your heart. Through the waves of beauty in your heart, touched by the sacred seas, you feel encouraged to share. You are in your sacred essence and inspiration encourages you to pursue your dreams. This is the great immensity of benevolence and grace. This is goodness radiating love and kindness that uplifts the world.

The Generosity encourages you to pursue your own inspired visions. It encourages you to pursue your own dreams. This energy is magnanimous and altruistic. It is kind, good, and lavish. It gives liberally to those who want to actively pursue inspiration.

This is the ultimate in largess. The universe is eternal and infinite, and so inspiration, while specific, is open and generous. There is more than enough to give. The universe gives with an open hand and an open heart. The bounty of vision and participation makes for a kindhearted expansion in which everyone can benefit.

The Generosity is open, fluid, responsive, and filled with the expansive frequencies of inspired love. There is no end to the gifts of inspiration. In this profuse generosity, you inspire inspiration. The flow of this energy invites people to play and gives them the opportunity to partake in that genius, the light, and the evolution. They see what you do, how you are, and they may want to join you because of the generous nature and true vision that you share. When you share these frequencies of inspiration, they touch others and trigger the light transfer, which is a gift to all.

Inspiration is bountiful and it flows through everything. You can benefit from this generosity because you can watch where it flows and how it is received. You can join with other people who appreciate altruism and are reciprocal in that appreciation. Generosity is not a handout. This nature of inspiration can open more opportunities for you and then you can open more opportunities for others. It is sharing your gifts in a way that is appropriate and filled with kindness.

Another benefit of this generosity is that other people can more easily find their own inspiration, because the energy you have, the vision you hold, inspires them to pursue their own magic. It's all so good!

The Generosity is blessedly reciprocal. If you reward your clients, you are working with generosity. If you acknowledge your customers, then you are paying them respect and sharing appreciation for their greateartedness to you. You can open up to inspired generosity, very simply give freely to charities, and share the love and spirit that is a bounty in your life.

Ask Yourself:

How can I be attuned to the generosity of inspiration and begin Living Inspired?

How can I be clear in my own life, and then share from a greater place? How can I share my myself and my work, my family, my clients, my business, and the world coming from a place of generosity?

When I know that inspiration is generous, where does the flow reveal itself to me? How do I expand on that?

Chapter 13:

Temple 7 ~
The Abundance

The depths of the night skies reveal the endless flow of stars and light shimmering over a distance you cannot calculate, you cannot measure, and you cannot hold. The universe wraps you in a space with no limits, no conceivable end or boundary. Your inspiration dances across the cosmos, laughing in the showers of stars and opportunities. The wealth, the opulence, and the affluence of the Divine bring more than you can say.

Inspiration creates *more*. The Abundance creates more inspiration. It opens you to possibilities, sometimes limitless possibilities. It can open you to possibilities into the future. There is more than enough. There is plenty. Knowing that inspiration is the power of good. Knowing that this goodness, this blessing is abundant encourages the light to travel and all hearts to shine.

The Abundance engages your thoughts, opens your interest, and helps you find your people. These people may be the ones who will help you share your vision. These people may be the ones who will support your vision through many different ways. These people may be lightbearers to the new innovation, unique gifts, and transformation that it will take for our world to transform its perceived limitations into abundance. These people may help our world evolve into a generous, good-hearted global community.

The Abundance is evident in our world. The earth showers us with beauty, grace, and love all of the time. Naturally, the most important thing is to see where abundance lives in your life. It's not all about money—the wealth of your life is abundance. This abundance also shows you and everyone of interest that there is more than you know. There is also more you can do with the positive energy, collection of ideas, brilliance of the systems, and the participation of the people you gather. This is abundance full on!

Explore your own wealth, in relationship to your inspiration. You may not realize that you do not trust the flow of abundance to support your vision and your dream. And while that may be understandable, it does not support The Abundance of the Divine One who shared this brilliance with you, in the heart of your soul, and who let you decide how you would share that with the world. That is faith in abundance. The Divine is sharing abundance with you in the form of inspiration.

This inspired vision, the ART, the Awakening, Revelation, and Transformation, you received comes from the fullness of abundance coming to you. You can see where that goes and how much you can share and receive.

Explore abundance as a model in your business. What feelings of opportunity do you bring to your clients, staff, and customers? What feelings and offerings of abundance do you give to your family and loved ones?

You can explore abundance as a model in your business. You can explore abundance as a model in your life. Living Inspired reinforces the abundance of the universe and encourage it to flow in your life.

Ask Yourself:

When you want to explore abundance in your business, look to see where does money and opportunity flow and where it does not. Is there an opening waiting for me? Is there a deterrent that I am avoiding?

What feelings of opportunity to I bring to my clients, staff, and customers? What feelings and offerings of abundance do I give to my family and loved ones?

You can explore abundance as a model in your life. What am I sharing that opens more for my spirit and my life? What professional training, what coaching, what help do I receive right now, that helps me know abundance in my life?

Where can I share the abundance? How can I increase the flow of abundance in my life and in the lives of others?

In the spirit of abundance, I'd like to ask you, what are you ready to give yourself right now?

Chapter 14:

Honoring the Sacred Lights

The seven temples of vibrating light are realms for new ways of knowing that vast resonance of inspiration. There is so much more to inspiration than you can ever imagine. All of these remarkable worlds and frequencies hold the vibrational spaces and attunements so you can experience the gifts of inspiration. I am sharing all of this with you so you can go beyond the illusions and misconceptions of inspiration and take on a whole new relationship with the divine messages available to you.

Each brilliant connection with inspiration, each of these Seven Temples of Vibrating Light, can interact with you. If your own life path is in harmony and your soul purpose and destiny is in the higher octave of alignment, then you may be able to enter each and every temple to expand your connection to the gifts of inspiration that you carry.

The seven temples of vibrating light are keys for your new way of exploring your world. Each attribute, each vibrational sequence creates a new relationship. When you sense the generosity coming though your experience of inspiration, you open yourself up to flow with it. Now inspiration connects you to generosity and you can include and express generosity in your message or wisdom. You can see how generosity enhances your inspiration. Maybe you feel more generous and are more giving. Maybe you feel generosity coming towards you and people bring you opportunities that are open and come from the heart.

Each attribute brings a new opportunity to expand inspiration in your life and in how you join the world. When you sense The Connection, you may sense that other people are seeing the light and catching it. Your path or message or blessing is spreading and connecting with others. Whether the message and vision of your own inspiration is spreading and reaching other like-minded people or the very nature and expression of inspiration is awakening other people, this brings spirit-led gifts into your world.

> **The Illumination** - It is an agent of change and transformation. It shines a positive light for those who are ready for a more brilliant path.

> **The Magnetism** - The Magnetism is an agent of reciprocal attraction. It is attracted to you because of your soul purpose, and you become part of this magnetic vortex of cosmic interest. When you resonate with this light, the universe helps you attract what enhances your inspiration.

The Reverberation - The Reverberation sends harmonic resonance into the world to echo your soul purpose. It helps you share your vision and generate joy and fulfillment. When you resonate with this light, the universe helps you broadcast a new harmony.

The Connection - The Connection joins you to the higher truth. Your light connects us to all light and holds higher aspects of relatedness. When you resonate with this light, the universe helps you create stronger and more beneficial connections to your purpose.

The Creation - The Creation embodies the brilliance. Out of the unformed comes beauty, in grace and in exuberance. This is the play of energies and possibilities. When you resonate with this light, the universe helps you create beyond what you have seen and know and this inspires others to see your greatness.

The Generosity - The Generosity is magnanimous, kind, lavish, and altruistic. It gives liberally. It is blessedly reciprocal. The universe gives with an open hand and an open heart. When you resonate with this light, the universe helps you experience the generosity of your own spirit and the gifts of others.

The Abundance - The Abundance creates more. It opens you to limitless possibilities. There is more than enough. There is plenty. When you resonate with this light, the universe helps you open and receive bountiful blessings.

Inspiration creates something new. Each engagement, every frequency, and every expression creates something new. Knowing this, experiencing and distinguishing this, brings you vibrant, meaningful, creative, and transformational ways to celebrate your life and enrich our world. When you actively engage with inspiration you are helping to change our world. You go from a passive, non-inclusive experience of uncertainty to an empowered, vibrant participation in uplifting our lives and our world.

PART 3:

Engage the Inspiration Experience

It's Jazz

Can you sing in circles of bliss?
Can you paint the rivers of wisdom?
Can you change the world on a trapeze?

Her inspiration was a dialogue, a conversation with the Divine
Poised at the edge of her mind and tickling her heart

The color of the night flowed through time like an illusion of the infinite
Every mask was shattered
Every fear exposed
Every transcendent chord tying her to past limitations was flying free in crescendo

Was there any wonder she felt so confident that she had no

clue what was going on?
Confident of the unknown
Confident of the road about to be taken
Only courage only heart knew more than she did

Bending time like a guitar string
The vibrations of her future self ricocheted light-filled
patterns that were soon to be born
Was this the different drummer?

Life is jazz,
Improvisation in multiple tempos of now
Bells and blossoms
Horns and guitars

And there is always fragrance
The scent leading her forward to the right place, right time,
right melody for change
Jazz life, soul matter, spirit mother
Dancing the rhythms of the goddess in steps of gladness
The essence, the vibration calling forth the fullness of being
There was more than enough joy.
Her purpose called and she answered
When destiny calls it's always good
To pick up the phone and pick up the tempo

Chapter 15:

Magic Message

L iving Inspired is the active expression of inspiration. It's important to take actions to pursue and discover your own inspiration. Not only is the Divine trying to communicate with you, through this rich and luscious vehicle of inspiration, but you can be at cause in your life. You can truly stop waiting for the light to shine on you. *Turn on the light.* Chase rainbows. Follow the unique rhythms.

Your inspiration is unique and specific to your soul, spirit, and self. The Divine is communicating with you. Every moment of all time, every planet in the heavens, and every experience of life converges in one moment so you can receive this guidance. Inspiration is the essence and power of the Divine connecting with you with a deeply personal, intimate, and powerful communication. Every cell of your body is shimmering with this light and vibration.

Inspiration touches the fullness of your being so you can share your unique expression in the world. It speaks to and illuminates your soul purpose. The substance, the vibration, the meaning is unique to you. You will feel a different resonance, a different nuance in the message because you are meant to experience it in relationship to your path and purpose. You can feel the power in this message. You feel shivers and you know that beauty is dear to you.

You will bring to the message the brilliance of your life and your purpose. You will understand and translate that message, the frequencies and revelation of the message, in the way that leads you to greater wisdom. That is another aspect of inspiration that is so brilliantly sublime. You are part of the message. You are part of the inspiration. The universe is incorporating you, your path, your brilliance, your destiny into the message that it sends to you.

The ART of Living Inspired, the Awakening, Revelation, and Transformation, is a pure gift that generates the changes in your life. Now you are moving into the resonance of your greater being. The ART of Living Inspired opens you to your greater purpose.

The Awakening calls your attention to the eternal moment. The Divine moves to connect with you and only you. This gathering of energy and attention calls to you. This is why you feel chills. This is when your own focus moves somewhere unique and distinct.

The Revelation opens this eternal moment into a universal embrace. This is why you feel joy. Life stops for a moment, an eternal moment, and you are moved. The vision, the message, the spiritual connection lights you. Concentric circles of blessing shower you and radiate from you. You are more than you know and more of who you are ready to become.

The Transformation uplifts your awareness and being to the greater part of your soul. You are resonating, shifting into a greater you, *"the more of you."* You can see how much bigger you are than the life you experience every day. Your future self, your enlightening vision is becoming clear.

You can choose to step forward into the vision. You are no longer passive—waiting, hoping, and praying to feel inspiration. This is the time to choose action. This is the opportunity for you to be Living Inspired.

Chapter 16:

Inspiration as Your Guide

Inspiration can be a guiding force in your life. That's when inspiration illuminates your world. That's when you shine. That's when the initial results of inspired transformation make a difference in your life.

After the ART of inspiration unfolds, then you are left with the whole vibration of it moving through you. You can feel the buzz. You can hold the excitement. And you can share the wisdom and insight. In the spiritual and vibrational terms, you resonate to a new level. Your personal energy and makeup has really shifted and accelerated. How this presents itself is that you can see, feel, and be more of who you are.

Now you can accept and affirm inspiration as your guide. This is not about actions you take. This is about changes you make.

You can integrate the changes and embrace a new vision. You can cherish and honor the shift in perspective and bring this with you as a new context in your life. You can treasure the gift and engage a different mode of thinking that expands your outlook. All of this unfolds from the inside out.

Inspiration can affect and change you in countless different ways:

It can influence specific areas of your personal life.

It can help you change things that you do or ways that you behave around loved ones and co-workers. Inspiration can show you ways that you can interact with others that will be more loving, honoring, and healing.

It can influence specific areas of your personal community life.

It can direct your attention to make changes that benefit others in your life. If you are a healer or work with other people in a community setting, then the inward changes can greatly influence how you are with people. It can bless and change your relationships and ways of being with other people. I'm not simply talking about being nicer. You may find a new way of listening or you may find that you have other ideas that will integrate with what you do and benefit other people without interacting with them.

It can influence specific areas of your professional life.

It can tap into circumstances that influence how you do business. It can influence and shift how you integrate certain systems and modalities. You may see the systems or departments of your business in new ways and begin to remodel your personal formats, which can, in turn, remodel your business systems. It can open new ways and perceptions that generate massive innovation and change, affecting your business and the world far into the future.

It can also influence our world.

When active inspiration is the guide, you move at a different tempo and vibration. In one aspect, just being that way, paying attention to the energy, wisdom, and truth of the inspiration will create ripples of change emanating through you into the world. Your contribution uplifts our world.

Remember, this is not about actions you take. This is about changes you make. From the inside out, you can influence communities, charities, and events. You will naturally choose to be involved with certain things, certain groups of people who uplift our world. This course is guided by the inspiration you receive and then spreads in a heartfelt influence in our world.

Inspiration guides your change.

Stop Waiting for Inspiration

People long for inspiration. They want to be inspired, to experience the clear divine hand acknowledging them, filling them with light and wonder. The encounter is exhilarating, enlightening, joyful, and profound. It appears as divine guidance or communication. Spirit communicates. The mysterious unfolds.

People are under the false impression that inspiration is a capricious and mercurial event. They think that inspiration happens to you, if you wait for it. So people wait for inspiration to happen. They wait for that magical moment when that spark ignites the beauty and elegance within them. But there is nothing active or proactive about waiting. That is a problem.

Most people will never be inspired because they are waiting for inspiration to grace their lives. Many people will never be able to work with the inspiration they receive because the seemingly arbitrary nature of inspiration does not overtly direct. Therefore, if people expect to wait for inspiration to happen and then assume that they will receive step-by-step directives for the Awakening, Revelation, and Transformation to take place, they will miss their true opportunities.

Here are the four most prominent and destructive false premises and delusional world views about inspiration:

Inspiration is an unpredictable whimsy of the Divine.

People cannot predict when inspiration will

happen. No matter how much a person may want inspiration to hit them, it remains elusive, fleeting, and unreliable. If a person is lucky, inspiration may show up one day. For some people inspiration never happens and there seems to be no reason why.

Inspiration requires patience and waiting.

People feel and believe that they have to wait for inspiration. They may prepare themselves, meditate, clear their space, and make room for it, but they are waiting for that blessed event.

Waiting and preparation does not guarantee that inspiration will happen. Many people wait and hope for inspiration to happen sometime, one day. Sometimes it does happen and sometimes it doesn't. Waiting for it is unproductive, frustrating, and ineffective.

Inspiration happens as an effect.

People believe that they are chosen by inspiration. They are struck by it. Usually people are inspired by something. It's a positive force, an enlightening experience.

It is unpredictable. Inspiration comes to them, happens to them, and influences them. They have no influence upon it. No matter how good, how clever, how creative, how intelligent, or how gifted they are, if a person assumes that inspiration just happens, they are at the mercy of a possibility.

Being inspired is a passive state.

As I mentioned, being inspired is passive. Even if a person is lucky enough to experience the blessings of inspiration, they are in a passive, receptive state. The state of being— *being inspired*—is a passive state because the energies and resonance of inspiration are happening to that person so they can receive the energies and wisdom.

This whole human world view is false, flawed, and deceptive. You wait to be inspired. You can even pray for it. You are inspired by something, someone, some circumstance. Or worse. You are still waiting for that fleeting experience, that magic moment to happen. Too much waiting!

You are about to change the world view, right now.

It's time to wake up and break apart this untruth and reveal the brilliance of inspiration. I want you to experience and know inspiration. I want you to feel the brilliance and the light. I am breaking apart the mythology and misconceptions. I go into this in greater depth in my Living Inspired trainings and my private coaching programs. There you receive the in-depth coaching, training, and vibrational alignments to connect to inspiration in very profound ways.

In this book, I am introducing you to new concepts of the rich realm of inspiration that has almost always been hidden from you, because you were waiting for it to show up. I have created a whole new concept, a whole new resonance for our world because I saw this was missing. By explaining this greater truth, I am liberating inspiration from being hostage to misconceptions. With the vibrations and blessings infused in this book, I am healing the pathways of energy so you can play a more active role in your destiny, not playing a role – playing fully in it – fully engaged. By reading this book, you are participating in changing the world view and opening new doors of expression and transformation.

I am invoking inspiration here, for you to experience it directly. I bring in these frequencies and illuminated wisdom, so you can know the greater fullness of its matrix and context.

Part of my own purpose is to bring you into higher alignment so you can fulfill your destiny. Unraveling the confusion brings you new ways of thinking and being and new opportunities to play your role in the world. As I help unravel each layer of misconception and deception, you will be able to take action to achieve your own destiny. Living Inspired is part of a path, part of a level of fulfillment that will bring you forward in powerful, joyful, and conscious ways.

Previously, I shared that inspiration is always positive. It is always uplifting and beneficial. This is immediate guidance for you. Seek the positive. Seek the openings. Identify the healing transformations. Some people are influenced by guidance that is not illuminated and does not bring higher levels of healing, peace, love, honor, appreciation, harmony, and light. That's not inspiration. Inspiration transforms you, adds more to your being and your evolution. It lights your path to beauty, soul purpose, and collective destiny.

Take this moment to explore the tips and exercises in Chapter 19. They will start you on the journey to Living Inspired. I invite you to contact me at **www.Lumari.com** and join the different ways you can take this to a whole new level.

If you could invite inspiration into your life, instead of passively waiting for it to come to you, would you?

If you could be fully present, know a greater part of who you are, and add to the healing, joy, and peace of our world, would you?

If you could live every day filled with the light of your own path and be guided by inspiration, would you?

You are Living Inspired when you actively pursue and receive the inspiration that helps you say yes to all three questions.

Chapter 17:

The Cosmic Happy Birthday Moment

Think of inspiration as a spiritual, cosmic happy birthday moment. Surprise!

You are doing what you do in a normal day. Then, *surprise*! The Divine calls you from the formless center of creative chaos. She sings a chorus of wonder in your ears. "Happy Birthday to you!" Spirit calls to you. Spirit begins to show you that this is your day. This is your moment to know something more, to experience a rush of wisdom. And, while She is singing the Happy Birthday song, you are opening the present! You are unwrapping the gifts of inspiration.

"Happy Birthday to you!"

Inspiration is a gift. The universe, the Divine connects with the cosmic alignment of our soul and sprit, and touches our mind and presence with a gift. The gift is inspiration. As you open this gift, you step into an indescribable garden filled with wonder that is yet to be revealed.

Inspiration is a magical moment. We are called to attention. We are called. The synthesis of our mind and spirit calls to us. We step into another layer of consciousness. In that moment our reality shifts and we open to receive light, wisdom, art, creativity, new perspectives, innovation, and greater brilliance. We are called to receive a unique realization, new information—a new way of seeing, knowing, or being.

The experience of being inspired is one of the most wonderful and desired experiences. It ranks right up there with love, joy, and freedom. When you experience inspiration, you expect to be moved. You expect to be transported to another world that kindles your imagination and directs your focus to something beyond what you know in the moment.

Inspiration is a divine influence. It is a communication and sacred revelation. Inspiration brings revelation. Something new and wondrous is unveiled. You are receiving this unique perception, vibration, and awakening. It is rarely a shared event. It is deeply personal and always uplifting.

Chapter 18:

It's Time to Turn the Light On!

I f you are not Living Inspired, then you are hiding out in the dark. You didn't know that before. You may have searched for your own light, wondered about your inspiration, and prayed for guidance. You need someone to shine a light on your life and continually hold that light higher and brighter. Now, I just want to share that this is bigger than you. There is really truth in the guidance that you cannot wait for the light to strike you. You have to turn on the light and be in action to Live Inspired.

Turn the light on! You need to shine a light on the darkness and let that brilliance be your next challenge. Follow the path of your inspiration and work with someone who can help you illuminate that path. This is a deep joy, a level of play that brings you into your greatness, while you help others find their own greatness.

You need a visionary coach who holds that focus, shines that light, and has achieved those heights so she can coach you to your own self-expression and destiny. The kind of transformation that you want is not achieved by working alone, in the dark. You need a visionary coach who can see you in the light and will bring you forward into a greater destiny and soul purpose. It's so important to work with trusted people who will help you shine a light on your gifts and support and empower you to bring your gifts into the world.

Many people say that if you don't share your gifts, the world will miss them. I agree and I have a very potent and personal experience of this. That's why I wrote this book and that's why I revealed the massive truth and frequencies of inspiration. This whole book is written to uncover the false ideas about inspiration and reveal the authentic descriptions, qualities, properties, and vibrational makeup of inspiration, so you can finally understand what you are missing.

What are you missing?

You are missing the moment to connect with a greater wisdom.

You are missing the level of awareness and energy to take actions that are meaningful to you.

You are missing the vision and vehicle to take your ideas, your insights, and your wisdom beyond the idea stages and into the world.

You are missing the choice and most efficient ways to make a difference in your life and this world.

When you do see the illusions and limitations superimposed on your beliefs, life, perceptions and on our reality you begin to see that living and acting from those limitations interferes with your greater gifts and purpose. With this wisdom and insight, you can make choices and take action to connect with the true energy and power of inspiration and shift into higher levels of your own greatness.

This book gives you a clear view into the real workings of inspiration, so you don't have to wait. You can go and get the inspiration to accomplish what is in your heart.

If you are a visionary, leader, creative, healer, innovator, or entrepreneur, and you can see the difference you can make in our world because of what you know now, I am honored that you are reading this book. You may have already experienced the light of inspiration and the brilliance that dawned in you to make the changes and create new visions for our world. You are in these professional positions because of the inspiration that was present and guided your life.

Now you are in a new position. By Living Inspired, you can take the actions to live your life in the calm, clear light of inspiration. You can engage inspiration and bring that perspective, vision, and wisdom into everything you do. The results are more clear, whole, productive, and fulfilling for you and everyone in your life.

You don't have to be a global leader, famous personality, brilliant scientist, revolutionary entrepreneur, or visionary artist to take actions to be Living Inspired and make a difference in your own life, in your family's life, and in our world. You are you. That is the most powerful place to stand. Inspiration meets you where you are. Then with that divine spotlight, you become "the more of you" and can take the actions you need, for the path that is right for you.

Every person can make a positive difference in this world. Every person can be a leader in her own way. Did you have people in your past who brought you the wisdom and guidance you needed to make changes or choices in your life? Did you have someone you looked up to or admired or trusted who helped you see more clearly and take the actions you needed to become more of who you are right now? Now you can actively be that person.

It doesn't matter what position you have in life, every position is a leadership position.

You can be an entrepreneur, a teacher, a cook, a mechanic, a designer, a gardener, a carpenter, or an accountant, and you can be a leader in your own way. You can be a healer, an artist, a bus driver, a counselor, a salesperson, a soldier, a student, a banker, or a software designer, and you can be a leader in your own way. You can be a mother, a father, a sister, a brother, a son, a daughter, a grandfather, a grandmother, an aunt, or an uncle, and you can be a leader in your own way.

Inspiration brings you the greater wisdom and connection to help others and change the world. You can change the world from the boardroom or the kitchen. You can lead from the stage or the classroom. When you understand the real truth and power of inspiration and you decide to get into inspired action, you can make a positive difference in people's lives whatever you do and wherever you are at the moment. You can even make a difference right now, at the moment of reading this book. (You can even make a difference right now, in this moment while reading this book.) If you make a choice to Live Inspired, and choose to take action on that decision, you can make a difference in this moment.

When I say we need you, when I say the world needs you, now you know I mean it. All of you have the opportunity to Live Inspired and take the actions to come from that divine place. It's time for you to step forward.

Let me ask you this: If you play small, if you wait and hope to be inspired instead of Living Inspired:

- How many people are you leaving behind?

- How many people will not be helped?

- How many lives will go unchanged?

- How many people will lose an opportunity in their own life because you didn't take the next steps to get the right coaching or guidance so you can be the gift in the most powerful, light-filled way?

Come out and play! Find a great visionary coach and teacher. Work with someone who sees your greatness and can help you achieve it. I certainly hope I am one of them.

Chapter 19:

Making Room for Inspiration

There are many dimensions and aspects of inspiration that we can engage in and practice. I understand that right now we are chosen by spirit to receive the blessings of inspiration, but there are ways to encourage inspiration to find you and ways that you can make yourself more available to inspiration.

I am taking you on a journey to end the myth of how the gods of inspiration find you, so that you have real access to the gifts and blessings of divine energy. Those of you who have experienced this gift know it is a beautiful experience. It lifts you. It stops the world and gives you a glimpse of something more—something transcendental—that then takes you on a journey that is uniquely yours.

Inspiration meets you in your own reality and then helps transform your experience so you can perceive more. Then you can seize upon the inspiration and use it as guidance to create, envision, guide, lead, or innovate your life and world. This book gives you a clear view into the real workings of inspiration, so you don't have to wait. You can go and get the inspiration to accomplish what is in your heart.

What's not to love about that? You can love everything about it—except waiting for it to happen in your life. If you want to be touched, moved, illuminated by inspiration, then you need to engage. You need to prepare. You need the mindset and the "spirit-set" to frame your journey. Please use the following three transformational tips to create your path to Living Inspired. These transformational tips are aligned with ART, the Awakening, Revelation, and Transformation of active inspiration.

Three Transformational Tips To Empower Your Journey Of Living Inspired

TIP NUMBER 1:
BE OPEN TO INSPIRATION ~ THE ENERGY OF AWAKENING

First, before taking in all of the great information I'm going to share, *be open to inspiration*. I know that this sounds very simple and you may even roll your eyes at me. That's fine. I'll just wink back at you.

Everyone may have different reasons that they want to be inspired. You want to be inspired because this will create a gracious momentum in your life. You want to feel the forward thinking, the passionate vision that captures your imagination and leads you to a new clarity and more. Be present to Awakening. (As mentioned in the ART section.)

If you want to experience that energy, then first, it's a great idea to be open.

Be open and non-judgmental to ideas or thoughts that show up. When you open to inspiration, many things can flow that were once thwarted. So you may have had ideas or thoughts that you felt were inconsequential or steeped in fantasy. In the past you may have ignored them or judged them. Now, just let them be. Let your ideas entertain you while you entertain them. Engage in conversation. Enjoy the personality of each thought, idea, impression, energy, and motion. No one said you need to marry these thoughts, but if you ignore or judge ideas and feelings before you even let them fly, then you are interrupting the flow. These thoughts may lead you to greater awakening and wisdom.

This is liberating. Isn't it time you gave yourself permission to play? Don't you want to entertain thoughts and ideas that are far-reaching, expansive, and extraordinary? Inspiration will take you on a journey that can unravel the hold on your status quo and allow you—encourage you—to open to "the *more* of you."

When you understand certain aspects or qualities of inspiration, like resonance, relationship, and frequency, you can invite inspiration into your life and open to it. Then you can actually create it.

TIP NUMBER 2:
SEIZE THE MOMENT ~
THE ENERGY OF REVELATION

Living Inspired is self- and spirit-generated. When you are Living Inspired, you are at cause. You initiate it. You create it. You have to seize the moment and be present in it. If the opportunity shows up, take it. If the world moves to a new perspective that only you can see, watch it. Be present to revelation. This is the Revelation in the ART.

Gratitude is very important. Be thankful the Divine showed up to share revelation with you. So many people wish they had inspiration in their lives, because inspiration can make life easier. You feel the guidance. You have a connection with spirit and presence and this gift is such an honor to receive.

I really feel the power of this tip and realization. In the entire universe, in every dimension of consciousness, the Divine still knows you and still wants to commune with you. Inspiration reveals that powerful truth and connection. You are welcome. You are honored. You have a purpose, and the Divine wants to share illumination with you.

So, right now, feel the gratitude and take a deep breath. Seize the moment and do this visualization:

Here's my image for you right now.

> You are standing in a breathtaking garden. All of the flowers are in bloom. The birds are singing their unique symphony and it's in perfect harmony with your mood.

The fragrance is delicious. The beauty is overflowing. The color is rich, and you are amazed at the feelings you have right now. You are grateful and happy and present to the wonders that life has right in this moment.

Now, visualize yourself taking a step into this garden. Put your arms out wide and take a step forward in this garden. Wrap your arms around the whole of it and embrace the whole garden with all of the trees, flowers, birds, and butterflies.

Embrace the music of the birds, the fragrance of the flowers, and the beauty of the vista.

Now, bring it all right inside your body. Take your arms and bring the whole thing right into your body, into your heart and into your soul.

Now take a breath and just experience yourself as a walking, breathing, dancing, laughing, singing garden.

Take another deep breath and hold this experience.

That is active inspiration. Living Inspired can be like that.

Inspiration is not a single occurrence. It is actually a state of being, an indwelling of energy and spiritual connection. I will reveal the multiple states and expressions of inspiration to give the full range of possibilities so you can connect with the magic moments.

TIP NUMBER 3:
INSPIRATION IS A GIFT ~
THE ENERGY OF TRANSFORMATION

Inspiration is a gift, whether you can self-generate inspiration or whether the universe gifts it to you.

Inspired gifts can bring you wisdom, insight, or understanding. You may receive gifts of seeing new systems and structures and organization. Those gifts can also bring discovery, connection, innovation, and maybe collaboration and community. The gifts themselves are vibrational. They are concepts, insights, flashes of light that announce a presence and present themselves. Be present to transformation.

When you see inspiration as a gift, then you are in the presence of greatness and connection. You receive the gift and create its place in the world. You make room for it in your life and in the world.

The Divine collaborates with you to bring your gifts forward. This changes your life. The powers of this gift, this divine acknowledgement of you in your deep self, along with the connection of this gift of inspiration, change your perceptions of the limitations in life.

The gift of inspiration and the transformation you receive crack open a window in the stuffy room of limitations—of preconceived notions. The window is open; fresh air is flowing through the room. You hear the morning birds singing. Soft golden light rises over the mountains. The day is filled with possibilities.

There are actions to take. This offering from the universe is now your offering to the world.

Inspiration is a benefit and offering from the universe to you to bring you more than you have, more than you know, and more than you understand is possible. What generosity! In the largeness of the universe, these gifts are here for you. This abundance and generosity is a reciprocal vibration you can receive and share.

INSPIRED ACTIONS

How are you going to carry this message in your life? You are also a factor in the how. How this inspiration gets out into the world relies on you. The inspiration—the creative expression or conversation of the universe, in the form of inspiration— has converged in your life. You have the freedom, innovation, and creativity to express it.

It's not about actions you take. It's about changes you make. When you presence the changes you make, you clearly see your transformation. Then the actions you take because of this transformation will bring you forward to greater purpose and inspiration.

How you hold yourself, how you hold this new wisdom will guide how you share it.

The ART, the Awakening, Revelation, and Transformation, shift your energy and your perspective. You can let the ART of inspiration be your guide. Follow the energy and be fully responsive to your inner compass. That's why inspiration came to you exactly in this way.

Actively engaging with your inspiration "turbo-charges" your energy, your ideas, and your life. With inspiration, that idea blasts forward. It carries energy. This makes the idea grow. It is bigger than it was. It opens up and expands with light and spirit. This makes it more desirable, more attractive, and more likely to succeed.

This is not manic and frenzied. It enhances your perspective. The focus and power of inspiration adds to your life. It fills out the energies and creates a concentrated wholeness. In this wholeness your unique gifts shine, your soul purpose becomes more profound, and you can feel and know a greater sense of yourself. Life feels on purpose.

Living Inspired supports your greatness, your true purpose in this world, and your gifts to this world.

Play in this right now. Play in the possibility that you will seize the opportunity to shift your perspective about inspiration from *being inspired* to *Living Inspired*.

Ask Yourself:

What can I do right now to take that next step?

What can I do right now to invite inspiration into my life?

What can I do right now to take the actions that enlighten my path of inspired exploration and contribution?

Will I take one step, right now, towards living inspired?

The End Is Only the Beginning

I Am the Dance of the Moon

I am the dance of the moon
Spinning dark shadows against the light
The tear that drips from my eye
Casts pools that move the tides of the oceans and hearts
To rhythms beyond the meaning of mortality.
As you spread your wings
You fly to me, the warmth of my watchfulness

I am the keeper of the dark
The secrets of your soul nestle safely within my craters
Like nests for the eggs of your dreams
Babies protected by twigs and mud

I am the reclaimer of aspiration
Each night I circle the skies
Scooping up the hopes beyond reach
Breathing light into the distance

Calling the whispers to my breast
Holding the prayers to my heart
Where they wait

These are my secrets
To dance the rhythm of immortality
To guard the secrets of being
To reclaim the hopes of the human heart
And to hold this sacred trust

Until the exalted dreams are fulfilled
Or until they are dreamt no more
Then together, we will spin into the darkness of a greater light
To inspire the universe, once again

Get more joy in your life!

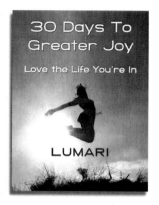

Free download!
30 DAYS TO GREATER JOY
Love the Life You're In

Discover simple, fun, actionable ways to bring more joy into your life!

- Move from mundane to magical
- Embrace your life and live inspired
- Take action to create more instant joy and ease

30 DAYS TO GREATER JOY

Get the free download here!
http://www.lumari.com/joy.html

Your joy momentum begins
as soon as you do!